ISBN 978-0-243-29610-1
PIBN 10792511

This book is a reproduction of an important historical work. Forgotten Books uses state-of-the-art technology to digitally reconstruct the work, preserving the original format whilst repairing imperfections present in the aged copy. In rare cases, an imperfection in the original, such as a blemish or missing page, may be replicated in our edition. We do, however, repair the vast majority of imperfections successfully; any imperfections that remain are intentionally left to preserve the state of such historical works.

1 MONTH OF
FREE
READING

at

www.ForgottenBooks.com

By purchasing this book you are eligible for one month membership to ForgottenBooks.com, giving you unlimited access to our entire collection of over 700,000 titles via our web site and mobile apps.

To claim your free month visit:

www.forgottenbooks.com/free792511

English
Français
Deutsche
Italiano
Español
Português

www.forgottenbooks.com

Mythology Photography **Fiction**
Fishing Christianity **Art** Cooking
Essays Buddhism Freemasonry
Medicine **Biology** Music **Ancient
Egypt** Evolution Carpentry Physics
Dance Geology **Mathematics** Fitness
Shakespeare **Folklore** Yoga Marketing
Confidence Immortality Biographies
Poetry **Psychology** Witchcraft
Electronics Chemistry History **Law**
Accounting **Philosophy** Anthropology
Alchemy Drama Quantum Mechanics
Atheism Sexual Health **Ancient History**
Entrepreneurship Languages Sport
Paleontology Needlework Islam
Metaphysics Investment Archaeology
Parenting Statistics Criminology
Motivational

𝔄 𝔏𝔦𝔣𝔢 𝔤𝔦𝔳𝔢𝔫 𝔣𝔬𝔯 𝔍𝔯𝔢𝔩𝔞𝔫𝔡

A SERMON

PREACHED AT THE

DEDICATION OF A MEMORIAL WINDOW

ERECTED BY MEN EMPLOYED IN THE IRON AND STEEL WORKS

TO THE LATE

LORD FREDERICK CAVENDISH

IN ST. JAMES'S CHURCH, BARROW-IN-FURNESS

ON ST. ANDREW'S DAY, 1882

BY THE REV.

STEPHEN E. GLADSTONE, M.A.

RECTOR OF HAWARDEN

Printed by Request

RIVINGTONS

WATERLOO PLACE, LONDON

MDCCCLXXXIII

[*Price Threepence*]

A LIFE GIVEN FOR IRELAND.

"Then said Jesus unto him, Go, and do thou likewise."—
St. Luke x. 37.

WHAT a record of joys and sorrows is the
history of human life on earth! As night
follows day, as sunshine breaks forth to dispel
the clouds, so is the heart of man wont to
feel the successive changes of the happiness
and the anxieties of life. Nay, even the
very heart which has been made bright with
joys knows at the selfsame moment "its own
bitterness." And how much deeper and
more piercing are the great sorrows of life
than its great joys. While one is rejoicing,
another is weeping. This very day we are
met together to try and glorify God for
events wholly differing in their character.
The three windows, unveiled this morning,

Parker and Co.

commemorate events, some of which were the occasion of deep joy and thankfulness, and others of the most heartrending grief. How different the occasions! a life spared, and a life taken; one life taken when not far off the term of three-score years and ten; another life suddenly cut down by cruel hands in the full vigour of manhood. So different, and yet it is so happy a blending: for whether our lot is one of joy or sorrow, we are to take that joy or sorrow as equally coming from the love of God. It is for His glory and our good. He alone can bless it. Apart from Him our truest earthly joy must fade and die; with Him to bless us, our keenest sorrows, borne as best we can in trust and patience, will but prepare us for the perfect life. Such souls as these which "sow in tears will reap in joy." May God bless those hearts who have been moved to mark their faith and love by the putting up of these memorial windows. To His eternal glory be they dedicated; and for ourselves let us not forget the events, the lives and deaths which they commemorate.

Too often do we take God's great gifts, and forget to thank Him : we turn to Him perhaps in trouble, but we forget Him in prosperity. Too often do we fail to profit by the lessons of a noble life, spent for God and for the souls God loves. Such heroes are living amongst us if only we have eyes to see and hearts to take notice ; living miracles, set before us even in this day, and in this country, in every rank and occupation, from the highest to the lowest—to teach us that the grace of God is still with His people, powerful to raise the natural man into the spiritual man, to hallow and train to their full growth and glory those powers and instincts which sin had corrupted, and which the world, the flesh, and the devil are ever striving to degrade and to destroy.

I see a correspondence between the lesson of this Festival of St. Andrew and the parable of the Good Samaritan, and the life of which

that window is commemorative. There is
the glorious life of self-sacrifice, of working
for the good of others, of doing one's duty
to one's neighbour however hard it may be:
—this lesson is contained in all three—can
I do better than ask you to consider it to-
night? St. Andrew was the disciple who
was always bringing others to our Lord.
Oh, how blessed a mark of a true, brave heart,
strong itself in faith and love, and longing
to draw others to know of the same pardon
and peace. Oh, brave manly hearts who
have met here to-night, strive hard to know
Jesus better yourselves, that you may do
something to comfort and raise the multitude
of immortal souls that are around you. One
thing only is wanting, and that is a heart
that has by true prayer and penitence found
Him itself. A Christian worthy of the name
must be one like St. Andrew, who brings
others to Christ, and by quiet perseverance
and brave example shows other men the
Lord and Saviour they have found.

And then, as for the Good Samaritan, who is He? Jesus Himself, the one perfect life; God, made Man for our sakes; He who was born for us, lived for us, suffered for us, died for us, rose from the dead for us, ascended for us, and even now is our High Priest within the veil, praying for us, and ever offering before the Father the oblation of Himself as the ground and strength of all the Church's prayers and blessings. Think of that devoted life. We know it so well, we hear it so often. Alas! it touches us so little. Its infinite pathos find our hearts so shallow and cold. Could we suddenly realize what it all was, could it rise up before our mind's eye as a statue long gazed on coming suddenly into life, oh, how it would thrill us through and through, and send us back to our daily lives with changed hearts, new determinations to fight against sin, and that strong love for Him which would enable us, in our poor degree, to "Go and do likewise." The sight of a picture of the crucifixion, or of the Head of Jesus crowned with thorns, has sometimes gone like a sword through some heart careless and untouched till then. Alas, how little the utter self-sacrifice of Jesus really touches our hearts and inspires our lives; and yet no life is noble, no act is noble that is not inspired by self-sacrifice. Nothing on earth can move us much to what is good and pure unless first we have been moved by the undying love of our Saviour. Truly He did love His enemies, even to the very end. He did bless them that persecuted Him. He spent His whole life for His faithless creatures. He died for those who despised, rejected, cruelly tormented, and shamefully slew Him. There is the sacrifice for our sins; thence we may have pardon and renewing grace. There is also the great Pattern for us to go and imitate. We must not only look at Christ crucified to be healed, but to get strength to live unselfishly, to live for others rather than ourselves, to make sacrifices of our own comfort, convenience; we must have our hearts warmed there with something of that enthusiastic love for man. And when any one is taken from our midst whose life has been a humble following of the One Perfect Life ; when after death we become, often for the first time, aware of how noble, how pure, how unselfish a life has been—then we shall do well, as on the present occasion, to study that life, to emulate its virtues, and to give glory to God for its faithfulness.

You will expect me to speak to you more particularly about this, looking to the occasion and the place. You knew something of his real worth—his simple goodness, his unaffected, manly, dutiful spirit, and his religious earnestness, none the less deep and real because it was so quiet and without show. Many of you were familiar with his frank and open face, his kind and courteous bearing. As Secretary to the Treasury his fair and impartial mind was found to be invaluable where all sorts of knotty points have to be referred and dealt with. All this, with entire devotion to his work and his great success in his official capacity, endeared him with a brother's love to his colleagues, and not less was he loved and respected by the permanent officials. It was devotion to his duty, it was an ardent love to do all he could for poor Ireland, that when suddenly called to a post of singular difficulty and real danger, made him ready to sacrifice himself, his own wishes, tastes, and comfort, wherever it was thought by those whom he trusted that he could do good. To be successful as Irish Secretary at that time was indeed a very unlikely thing for any one. But not even his self-mistrust, any more than his natural shrinking from such a duty, made him hesitate. A spirit, nobly proud, dreads failure more than death. He knew he might fail : some said he would. The papers, on the day he left his home for Ireland, were full of all sorts of criticisms, many of them idle. How little did those writers know the way that was before him. He was destined in less than one day's time to become, by the sacrifice of his life-blood, one of the chief causes of the gradual restoration of peace and order, at a moment of great danger. To go there was an act of real self-denial to him. At one moment, when it was thought he would not be required to go, he expressed his great sense of relief. I believe he was quite aware of the personal danger he incurred, though he would not make anything of it for the sake of those he loved and trusted. Straight forward he went, when called to go; and what encouraged him amongst other things was his real ambition to help the Irish people, and his ready sympathy with many of their aspirations. He had not lost confidence in them; he believed the heart of Ireland was sound, though terrible symptoms of disease had appeared.

You know he left London on Friday night, May 5th; and on Saturday, the very day he landed, with his heart full of doing

good, anxious not to lose a single moment
even then, he set himself down to work, at
Dublin Castle, on some most important
points. It was this very eagerness to do
his duty that led to his desire for extending
his walk in the evening of that day which
proved his last. Ten or twelve hours after
landing, with only one desire in his heart,
to help a deeply suffering country, you know
how, unarmed, unprotected, he fell beneath
the murderous attack of a number of armed
men, together with his companion, another
noble heart, also honoured and beloved by
all who knew him. Alas! how often men
know not their best friends. Cowardly and
atrocious as was that attack beyond all
words, can we suppose it would have been
made if those men, bad and brutal as they
were, had known what was really in those
true hearts? You may know that *his* life,
in all probability, according to evidence obtained, was not aimed at; though this hardly
mitigates the ferocity of that crime which

rang throughout the civilized world ; and, alas! it has to be added that in the worst quarters of the city there was, at least at the first, considerable rejoicing at his death. And yet, could we look through the veil which for a while separates us from eternity, who can doubt that the same love of the people, the same trust in their real soundness at heart, which beat in his heart, when alive, still is filling his soul after death ? Great indeed was the outburst of deep indignation throughout the country, and of course not least in England—happily an indignation, a horror held in check as usual by the English self-restraint. And, thank God! equally great was the burning sense of shame and horror in Irish hearts when they awoke to what had been done. Many were the signs of this widespread and deep grief. You may remember, for example, the account of the priest in County Galway, reading that most touching letter of Lady Frederick Cavendish to a weeping congregation.

Though these two murders were not, indeed, worse than others, yet the surrounding circumstances made them more terribly sad, and they are said by those who best know to have been the turning-point in the last terrible history of crime and outrage. It was, in fact, these deaths which woke up the people from their apathy about crime. Since that dreadful 6th of May it is a fact that crimes of all sorts have steadily declined, both in the number and in the quality of the acts. And though every now and then we are still startled by a new act of horror (as, alas! has been the case this very week), it is reassuring to know that the country is returning to a state of peace, and of greatly increased prosperity. The return of agrarian outrages was 531 for March last. For June the number was reduced to 283, and in September to 131 (half of which were threatening letters). Looking at the matter from another point of view, we find that last September there were 59 actual offences against persons, property, and the public peace, as against 225 twelve months before. Further notice that in March last 587 men were in prison merely on suspicion, whereas now there are none. We were further told the other day by the present Irish Secretary that from the reports of those in authority in the disturbed districts, it was certain that the state of feeling from which crime sprang is materially improving. These men, who know the country well, all say that the relations between landlord and tenant are improved, that rents are being fairly paid, and that intimidation is decreasing. Mr. Davitt himself regretfully indicates by his speeches that agitation is dying out because the people of Ireland imagine they have got justice by the Land and Arrears Acts.

It was to help Ireland that he went; and now can we doubt for a moment that, in a manner little expected, he has helped Ireland in the most signal way? His life has been

sacrificed to the fierce hatreds which have
been the awful result of centuries of the
horribly wicked misrule of England.   But
Irish hearts now know what he was; and
the memory of that terrible deed must still
live to do something towards softening the
hardest hearts.   The desolation of a happy
home, the awful blank left by his death,
the piteous character of all the circumstances,
all go to show how great a sacrifice it has
been.   You know how all his unselfish
devotion to duty, all the risks which he so
cheerfully undertook, when asked to go,
were shared by his wife.   His death has
darkened a bright life indeed, but you know
she has given him up freely to God in the
comfort alone of the thought that his death
was for the good of the country he wished
to serve.   Oh, do not let us cease to pray for
her in her great sorrow, which in some ways
must become greater still by the lapse of
time.

Wonderful are the ways of God; we know

not His mind. That death has deprived the Queen and country of a faithful servant indeed. It has removed from public life a pure soul, single-hearted, and full of gentleness, yet of inflexible principle, and full of future promise. You may know, but I of course know far better, what a terrible, an irreparable, loss it has been to the chief adviser of the Crown, on whose head there has devolved such an enormous weight of responsibility. The Prime Minister's appreciation of him as a man, as a Christian, and of his work, was always intense. To see him was always a very real refreshment to his mind. None could have been a truer friend and wiser counsellor, though so much younger in years. And you need not to be told that, where a man has to bear such a great burden on his shoulders, as the Prime Minister has, a true-hearted, generous, wise sympathy, such as he had invariably found in his younger colleague, is a source of comfort and joy beyond what words can tell. It was a very

real grief to him when he felt it his duty for
the public good to ask Lord Frederick Cavendish to go to Ireland; for it was like losing
a right hand.

But great as is his personal loss, the public
loss is far greater. The State can ill spare
such men — men who put principle first,
interest afterwards; who are known to be
inflexibly just; who will neither give nor
take flattery; men who by their thorough-
going honesty raise political questions out of
the low atmosphere into which they are too
often dragged into higher, purer air; men
who take pains in forming their opinions and
have the courage to stand by them, however
unpopular they may at times chance to be;
men with moral backbone, as well as good
intellect—such men in public life amongst
the rising generation can ill be spared, and
such a one was be. All this was felt, and
the feeling was made evident not only at the
striking scene of the solemn Christian funeral,
but in the House of Commons—the House

crowded, pale, silent, but most really and deeply agitated, especially the Irish leader and the Irish members.

How powerfully on such occasions is the noble saying felt to be deeply true, "He being dead, yet speaketh." That life, that unselfish labour for others, that death, speaks, and will speak to us and to all true patriotic hearts. It speaks of that same love of others which the beautiful window tells of in the figure of the Good Samaritan; the same noble love which is greater than all other love, which, when called on to go, goes into difficulty and danger, with the one ambition of doing good—yes, that love which makes a true man ready to lay down his own life for his friends. Oh, Irish hearts, he died for you, as well as by the hands of cruel men amongst you. Oh, English hearts, he died for the wicked tyranny, the awful selfishness, the bloody cruelty of many of your forefathers. Let both countries be conscience-stricken with a common shame and sorrow;

and may God grant that so stricken, they may be drawn nearer together, with mutual forbearance, and patient considerateness : and then that death will indeed not have been in vain.

And for ourselves, let that life and death do its work within us. These events are allowed to happen to arouse us from our sloth and sins, and to inspire us with high thoughts of serving our God and our country. "Go, and do thou likewise," is what this life and death says to us. That window speaks the same words. And we can, each of us, in our way, make a true answer to this appeal. There is not one of us who might not be able to do, even where we are, great things for our God and our country. Manfully to do our work—whatever that work may be— bravely to witness for Christ against every form of vice—particularly to try and do little deeds of kindness, of Christian neigh- bourliness, to others—and to go on day after day setting an example to those around

us, in the thought of the great reward in
store for him who has lived unselfishly and
helped his brethren—all this is as much
open to the poor labourer as to the noble-
man ; yes, to the little child even, to the
sick and infirm, to the sad and suffering.
For we are not our own : ourselves redeemed
by the blood of God in the flesh, we owe it
to Him to love and labour for those He died
to save.   To live merely for our own enjoy-
ment, however free even of open sin we may
be, is an ignoble, a despicable life ; whereas
to minister to others' needs, to comfort the
sufferers, to help the falling and fallen, to
protect with true British chivalry the weaker
ones, to spend and be spent for these high
purposes, is the way to raise human nature
to those glorious heights of true and eternal
nobleness which, through Jesus Christ our
Saviour, now properly belong to it.   Such
lessons of noble devotion let us try and learn,
every one of us.   Others have learnt them ;
let us do the same.

Other Men's Labour.

A SERMON

ON THE DEATH OF THE

REV. E. B. PUSEY, D.D.

PREACHED AT

ST. GILES' CHURCH, OXFORD,

On the Sixteenth Sunday after Trinity,

SEPTEMBER 24, 1882,

BY THE

REV. R. ST. JOHN TYRWHITT, M.A.

FORMERLY SENIOR STUDENT AND RHETORIC READER
OF CHRIST CHURCH, OXFORD.

society is become corrupt; the light that is in it is become darkness; the leaven that leavens it is not the Divine leaven pf the Gospel, but that of worldliness, selfishness, sensuality, and wickedness; therefore all these miseries—the necessary fruits of sin—come upon it. The Gospel is called the light of the world, the salt that is to keep it from corruption, the leaven that is to leaven all man's life, and how awfully does history and the course of the Divine judgements show that it is so indeed; for if in any nation that light is put "under a bushel," or is not set on a sufficient "candlestick" so that all who come in may see it, then more and more do we *see* darkness of every kind covering it. And "if the light that is in it be darkness," if what pretends to ▓▓▓ristianity is, for the most part, some frightful perversion of it, "how ▓▓▓ is that darkness!" And if any "body" of society of men is ▓▓▓ with that salt, how visibly does it decay and become utterly co▓▓▓ "I▓▓ salt have lost its savour" —if the teachers and lea▓▓rs of ▓blic op▓▓on in any nation have become worldly—"wherewith shall it be salted?" "It is thenceforth good for nothing but to be cast out and trodden under foot of men." He must be blind who does not, by this time, perceive how entirely it is one principle, and one only which "has the promise of the life that now is, as well as of that which is to come"—namely, real and true Christian faith—one GOD, one only who in the end rules this as well as all other worlds—namely, GOD manifest in CHRIST. Where that faith is not, everything sooner or later decays—"it carries within itself the germs of its own dissolution." All spiritual food is useless or poisonous that is not leavened with this; all light is darkness that is not borrowed from and illumined with this. If we would make our education worth anything at all—if we would have teachers who shall do any good and not wide-spreading harm—if we would teach politics in any way that shall not be poisonous—all must be leavened with this leaven of real uncorrupted Christianity. It is not necessary only, or chiefly, that the teachers should be men who profess Christianity as their declared creed, nor yet that the doctrines of the Bible should be taught at times, but the main point is, that true uncorrupted Christianity should be the leaven, leavening the whole character of the teacher, and giving its savour to the whole doctrine taught about everything. This is the sole and only true remedy for all our ills: "this *is*" *now*—just as much as shall be hereafter—"life eternal to know Thee the only true GOD and JESUS CHRIST whom Thou hast sent." Leaven a nation with this faith and it will come soon to "glory, honour, and immortality;" take away this, or turn the faith which ought to be "leaven, leavening the whole lump"—leavening all politics, philosophy, and wisdom into a dead stone separate from all life —and in the end it will come to sure destruction and shame—to "indignation and wrath, tribulation, and anguish." If men will not believe this by *faith* in GOD's word, they will be compelled sooner or later to

CPSIA information can be obtained
at www.ICGtesting.com
Printed in the USA
BVHW071110080119
537312BV00021B/953/P